ALSO BY ROSALIND KILKENNY MCLYMONT

Middle Ground

Africa: Strictly Business,
The Steady March to Prosperity

The Guyana Contract

With Rosalind Kilkenny McLymont

In the Eye of the Storm:
My Time As Chairman of Bank Of America
During the Country's Worst Financial Crisis

(Walter E. Massey Memoir)

LIFTED!

150 QUOTES THAT MOTIVATE
HIGHLY SUCCESSFUL BLACK WOMEN

Rosalind Kilkenny McLymont

Rosalind Kilkenny McLymont
New York

United Writers Press
Asheville, NC

LIFTED!
150 Quotes That Motivate Highly Successful Black Women

First Edition

Published in the United States by:
Rosalind Kilkenny McLymont
and United Writers Press
www.uwpnew.com

ISBN: 978-1-961813-40-3 (trade paperback)
ISBN: 978-1-961813-41-0 (casebound)

Library of Congress Control Number: 2023916021

Art Work by Movement Graffiti
Cover Design & Layout by United Writers Press

The cover art is derived from a macro photograph of barkcloth, traditionally created and worn by the Baganda people of Uganda, especially those in the royal family. This technique of stripping and beating the bark of the Mutuba tree with mallets until soft, for use in making clothes and other objects, predates the invention of weaving.

Printed in the United States.

For The great-granddaughters

of Alfred and Ruby Kilkenny

Dylan

Naya

Brooklyn

Secret

Esther

Rachel

INTRODUCTION

The quotations in this book were selected from personal statements submitted to *The Network Journal* by recipients of the magazine's "25 Influential Black Women in Business" annual awards from 2000 to 2021.

Launched in 1999, the awards highlight and honor often-unacknowledged achievements of Black women in the United States. The typical award recipient is an entrepreneur or a woman entrusted with significant decision-making authority in a corporate, not-for-profit, academic, or healthcare organization, or in public office. And she has a track record of providing leadership and support to her community. Award recipients reside in the United States, but they represent national and cultural origins spanning the U.S., Africa and communities of people of African descent worldwide.

As executive editor of *The Network Journal*, I am privileged to review the personal statements of these extraordinary women. The motivating words they cite attest to their universal soul, one that values historical and present-day counsel, irrespective of geographic, ethnic or cultural origin, whether from the famous or the unknown. I hope readers of this book draw as much from these words as the women who are lifted by them.

Rosalind Kilkenny McLymont
New York
2023

LIFTED!

150 QUOTES THAT MOTIVATE
HIGHLY SUCCESSFUL BLACK WOMEN

"What you can believe, you can achieve."

NAPOLEON HILL

"If you fail to go within, you'll go without."

VICTOR FRANKL

"Adversity is a springboard to great achievement."

HARVEY MACKAY

"Success is a journey, not a destination."

ARTHUR ASHE, JR.

"Life has two rules. Rule Number One: Never quit. Rule Number Two: Always remember Rule Number One."

DUKE ELLINGTON

"Risk more than others think safe. Dream more than others think practical. Expect more than others think is possible."

CLAUDE THOMAS BISSELL

"When my life is moving according to divine order, it is so much better than what I try to orchestrate myself."

ALICE M. DEAR

"If you always do what you've always done, you'll always get what you've always got."

HENRY FORD

"It is better to look ahead and prepare than to look back and regret."

JACKIE JOYNER-KERSEE

"There is no such thing as an average life, only limited vision."

PHYLLIS G. WOOLEY

"Your candle loses nothing when you light another's."

JAMES KELLER

"We can make a living by what we get. We can make a life by what we give."

SIR WINSTON CHURCHILL

"If you don't understand the history of where you've been, you cannot possibly understand the future of where you're going."

MARIA L. JOHNSON

"Faith is believing in advance what will only make sense in reverse."

PHILIP YANCEY

"No one can make you feel inferior without your consent."

ELEANOR ROOSEVELT

"Make the best of what is in your power, and take the rest as it happens."

EPICTETUS

"**Obstacles are what you see when you take your eyes off the goal.**"

HENRY FORD

"Trust your instincts. Listen to your inner voice. It will not lead you in the wrong direction."

JACQUELINE W. SALES

"Whatever you can do or dream you can do, begin it!"

JOHANN WOLFGANG VON GOETHE

"If you don't go after what you want, you'll never have it. If you don't ask, the answer is always no. If you don't step forward, you're always in the same place."

NORA ROBERTS

"A sure way for one to lift himself up is by helping to lift someone else."

BOOKER T. WASHINGTON

"**Optimism is the faith that leads to achievement. Nothing can be done without hope and confidence.**"

HELEN KELLER

"There are no secrets to success. It is the result of preparation, hard work and learning from failure."

COLIN POWELL

" **Creativity is God's gift to you. What you do with it is your gift to God.** "

BOB MOAWAD

"The good you do today may be quickly forgotten, but the impact of what you do will never disappear."

KATHERINE GISCOMBE

"There is no passion to be found in playing small, in settling for a life that is less than the one you are capable of living."

NELSON MANDELA

"Service is the rent
you pay for living."

MARIAN WRIGHT EDELMAN

"Excellence is never an accident: it is the result of high intention, effort, intelligent direction, skillful execution."

ARISTOTLE

"Progress lies not
in enhancing what
is, but in advancing
toward what will be."

KHALIL GIBRAN

"Our deepest fear is not that we are inadequate. Our deepest fear is that we are powerful beyond measure."

NELSON MANDELA

"A person has to
be willing to make
a mistake. Find a
way to step outside
their comfort zone
and be there long
enough to experience
something new."

LISA A. BING

"The quickest way to get ahead is to push yourself there."

JOLI C. COOPER

"A leader takes people where they want to go. A great leader takes people where they don't necessarily want to go, but ought to be."

ROSALYNN CARTER

"**Who you are is speaking so loudly that I can't hear what you're saying.**"

RALPH WALDO EMERSON

"It is the energy that you put out into the Universe that comes back to you whether in the short term or long term-but it eventually does."

THE SECRET

"To whom much is given, much will be required; and from the one to whom much has been entrusted, even more will be demanded."

LUKE 12: 48-49

"Never, never, never quit."

SIR WINSTON CHURCHILL

"Ability is what you're capable of doing; Motivation determines what you do, and Attitude determines how well you do it."

"You can never be happy living someone else's dream."

OPRAH WINFREY

"**Luck is what happens when preparation meets opportunity.**"

SENECA

"If you compare yourself with others, you may become vain or bitter; for always there will be greater and lesser persons than yourself. Enjoy your achievements as well as your plans."

DESIDERATA

"I can do all things through Christ which strengthens me."

PHILIPPIANS 4:13

"I have learned that you shouldn't go through life with a catcher's mitt on both hands; you need to be able to throw something back."

MAYA ANGELOU

"You have been given this day to use as you will. You can waste it or use it for good."

MAC ANDERSON

"The ultimate measure of a man is not where he stands in moments of comfort and convenience, but where he stands at times of challenge and controversy."

"Tenderness and kindness are not signs of weakness and despair, but manifestations of strength and resolutions."

KHALIL GIBRAN

"The will of God will never take you where the grace of God will not protect you."

BILLY GRAHAM

"Listen to the whispers before they become screams."

NATIVE AMERICAN PROVERB

"I am not interested in power for power's sake, but I am interested in power that is moral, that is right, and that is good."

MARTIN LUTHER KING, JR.

"I have learned that people will forget what you said, people will forget what you did, but people will never forget how you made them feel."

MAYA ANGELOU

"Great minds have purposes, others have wishes."

WASHINGTON IRVING

"Challenges are gifts that force us to search for a new center of gravity. Don't fight them. Just find a different way to stand."

OPRAH WINFREY

"Don't sweat the small stuff."

RICHARD CARLSON

"Lead, follow, or get out of the way."

THOMAS PAINE

"Being powerful is like being a lady. If you have to tell people you are, you aren't. "

MARGARET THATCHER

"If you produce, people will take you seriously."

MUHAMMAD ALI

"**Adversity causes some men to break, others to break records.**"

W.A. WARD

"Faith is the substance of things hoped for, the evidence of things not seen."

HEBREWS 11:1

"Bloom where you are planted."

MARY ENGELBREIT

"Trust in the Lord with all thine heart; and lean not to thine own understanding. In all thy ways acknowledge him and he shall direct thy paths."

PROVERBS 3: 5-6

"There are few misfortunes in this world that you cannot turn into a personal triumph if you have the iron will and the necessary skill."

NELSON MANDELA

"For I know the plans I have for you," declares the Lord, **"plans to prosper you and not to harm you, plans to give you hope and future."**

JEREMIAH 29:11

"God grant me the serenity to accept the things I cannot change, courage to change the things I can, and wisdom to know the difference."

THE SERENITY PRAYER

"My philosophy is that not only are you responsible for your life, but doing the best at this moment puts you in the best place for the next moment."

"How much further can I stretch to reach my full potential?"

OPRAH WINFREY

"The ultimate measure of a man is not where he stands in moments of comfort, but where he stands at times of challenge and controversy."

MARTIN LUTHER KING, JR.

"**Success is empty when you are not living on purpose.**"

VALORIE BURTON

"Nothing is worth more than this day."

JOHANN WOLFGANG VON GOETHE

"Attitude determines altitude."

SANDRA BOOKMAN

"Don't make money your goal. Instead pursue the things you love doing and then do them so well that people can't take their eyes off of you."

MAYA ANGELOU

"**Ask for what you want and be prepared to get it.**"

MAYA ANGELOU

"As we are liberated from our own fear, our presence automatically liberates others."

MARIANNE WILLIAMSON

"It's amazing how much can be accomplished if no one cares who gets the credit."

HARRY S. TRUMAN

"There is nothing enlightened about shrinking so that other people won't feel insecure around you."

MARIANNE WILLIAMSON

"Your work is going to be a large part of your life, and the only way to be truly satisfied is to do what you believe is great work. And the only way to do great work is to love what you do."

STEVE JOBS

"A sense of humor...
is needed armor. Joy
in one's heart and
some laughter on
one's lips is a sign
that the person down
deep has a pretty
good grasp of life."

HUGH SIDNEY

"When you fall in life, don't look at where you fell—look at where you slipped."

AFRICAN PROVERB

"When someone shows you who they are, believe them the first time."

MAYA ANGELOU

"Cows run away from the storm while the buffalo charges toward it, and gets through it quicker. Whenever I'm confronted with a tough challenge...I become the buffalo."

WILMA MANKILLER

"Bring more to the table than your appetite."

AFRICAN PROVERB

"Do not judge me by my successes, judge me by how many times I fell down and got back up again."

NELSON MANDELA

"Don't listen to those who say you can't. Listen to the voice inside yourself that says, 'I can.'"

SHIRLEY CHISHOLM

"The greatest danger for most of us is not that our aim is too high and we miss it, but that it is too low and we reach it."

"It is not the critic who counts … The credit belongs to the man who is actually in the arena."

THEODORE ROOSEVELT

"Every great dream begins with a dreamer. "

HARRIET TUBMAN

"It is better to be prepared for an opportunity and not have one, than have one and not be prepared."

WHITNEY YOUNG, JR.

"Success usually comes to those who are too busy to be looking for it."

HENRY DAVID THOREAU

"The price of success is hard work, dedication to the job at hand, and the determination that whether we win or lose, we have applied the best of ourselves to the task at hand."

VINCE LOMBARDI

"Whoever debases others is debasing himself."

JAMES BALDWIN

"Faith is taking the first step even when you don't see the whole staircase."

MARTIN LUTHER KING, JR.

**"Life is a succession
of lessons which
must be lived to
be understood."**

RALPH WALDO EMERSON

**"Do not go where
the path may lead...
go instead where
there is no path
and leave a trail."**

RALPH WALDO EMERSON

"The world is made of sheep and wolves. Wolves eat sheep and Super Wolves eat wolves. Which do you want to be?"

CHARLES E. SHELTON

"**A good head and a good heart are always a formidable combination.**"

NELSON MANDELA

"It always seems impossible until it's done."

NELSON MANDELA

"Life is not about waiting for the storm to pass…it's about learning to dance in the rain."

VIVIAN GREENE

"To know even one life has breathed easier because you have lived. This is to have succeeded."

RALPH WALDO EMERSON

“Learn from yesterday, live for today and hope for tomorrow. The important thing is to not stop questioning. Curiosity has its own reason for existing.”

ALBERT EINSTEIN

"Leave the ladder down for others to follow."

RONALD HARMON BROWN

"The only person you are destined to become is the person you decide to be."

RALPH WALDO EMERSON

"**Moments are useless, trifled away; so work while you work and play while you play.**"

M.A. STODART

"If you don't like something, change it. If you can't change it, change your attitude."

MAYA ANGELOU

"In the end, it's not the years in your life that count. It's the life in your years."

ABRAHAM LINCOLN

"Here is my secret. It is very simple. It is only with the heart that one can see rightly. What is essential is invisible to the eye."

ANTOINE DE SAINT EXUPERY

"Hearts are the strongest when they beat in response to noble ideals."

RALPH BUNCHE

"Success is what you do for yourself. Greatness is what you do for others. Is success your standard, or is greatness your goal?"

RANDAL PINKETT

"**Men with good intentions make promises, but men with good character keep them.**"

A.R. BERNARD

"We are all faced with a series of great opportunities, brilliantly disguised as impossible situations."

"There is only one thing that makes a dream impossible to achieve: the fear of failure."

PAULO COELHO

"When you have come to the edge of all light that you know, and are about to drop off into the darkness of the unknown, Faith is knowing one of two things will happen:

there will be
something solid to
stand on or you will
be taught to fly. **"**

PATRICK OVERTON

"People don't care how much you know until they know how much you care."

UNKNOWN

" The greatness of humanity is not in being human, but in being humane. "

MAHATMA GANDHI

"If you don't go after what you want, you'll never have it. If you don't ask, the answer is always no. If you don't step forward, you're always in the same place."

"We teach what we know, but we reproduce what we are."

JOHN MAXWELL

"**Our greatest glory is not in never failing, but in rising every time we fall.**"

CONFUCIUS

"Success is liking yourself, liking what you do, and liking how you do it."

MAYA ANGELOU

"May your choices reflect your hopes, not your fears."

NELSON MANDELA

"When I stand before God at the end of my life without a single bit of talent left, I like to say "God I used everything you gave me."

ERMA BOMBECK

"Be anxious for nothing, but in everything by prayer and supplication, with thanksgiving, let your requests be made known to God."

PHILIPPIANS 4:6

" **The only place success comes before work is in the dictionary.** "

VINCE LOMBARDI

"There is no growth in the comfort zone and no comfort in the growth zone!"

WILL LINSSEN

"Cowardice asks the question, is it safe? Expediency asks the question, is it politics? Vanity asks the question, is it popular? But, conscience asks the question, is it right?"

"**Be bold, and mighty forces will come to your aid.**"

BASIL KING

"Never get so busy making a living that you forget to make a life!"

DOLLY PARTON

"Control your own destiny or someone else will."

JACK WELCH

"Be fearless in the pursuit of what sets your soul on fire."

JENNIFER LEE

"You have brains in your head. You have feet in your shoes. You can steer yourself in any direction you choose. You're on your own. And you know what you know.

And YOU are the one who'll decide where to go. "

DR. SEUSS

"Success is when smarts and an empowering attitude overcome hurdle after hurdle, not only to survive 'the wolves,'

but to arrive with pride at a secure place with the respect of those who matter. "

BARBARA KUSHNER

"It took me a long time to develop my voice and now that I have it, I am not going to be silent."

MADELEINE ALBRIGHT

"A dream doesn't become reality through magic; it takes sweat, determination and hard work."

COLIN POWELL

"It's not enough to follow your dreams. We must chase them."

TENESHIA JACKSON WARNER

"If not you, then who? If not now, then when?"

"**Empowerment comes from being confident in your own female skin, no matter if you are not seen as cute or fashionable by the masses.**"

MAYA ANGELOU

"Tell me who your friends are and I'll tell you who you are."

MIGUEL DE CERVANTES

"Create the highest, grandest vision possible for your life, because you become what you believe."

OPRAH WINFREY

"Without leaps of imagination, or dreaming, we lose the excitement of possibilities. Dreaming after all, is a form of planning."

GLORIA STEINEM

"**Finally, brothers and sisters: Whatever is true, whatever is noble, whatever is right, whatever is pure, whatever is**

lovely, whatever
is admirable—if
anything is excellent
or praiseworthy—
think about such
things. "

PHILIPPIANS 4:8

"If you're always trying to be normal, you will never know how amazing you can be."

MAYA ANGELOU

"Not that I speak in respect of want: for I have learned, in whatsoever state I am, therewith to be content."

PHILIPPIANS 4:11

"Watch your thoughts
they become words;
watch your words,
they become actions;
watch your actions,
they become habits;
watch your habits,

they become your character; watch your character, it becomes your destiny. **"**

CHINESE PROVERB

"Don't worry about the level of individual prominence you have achieved; worry about the individuals you have helped become better people."

CLAYTON CHRISTENSEN

"Live your life as a powerful example, not as an example of power."

JOAN M. PRINCE, PH.D.

"Our deepest fear is that we are powerful beyond measure. It is our light, not our darkness that most frightens us. We ask ourselves,

Who am I to
be brilliant,
gorgeous, talented,
and fabulous?
Actually, who are
you *not* to be?**

MARIANNE WILLIAMSON

"To be human, is to have the innate power to materialize the invisible. That is, we possess a gift that allows us to create a future that does not yet exist."

ERWIN MACMANOS

"The best way to find yourself, is to lose yourself in the service of others."

MAHATMA GANDHI

"Life is no brief candle for me. It is a sort of splendid torch which I have got hold of for the moment, and I want to make

it burn as brightly
as possible before
handing it on to
future generations. **"**

GEORGE BERNARD SHAW

"To build a better world we need to replace the patchwork of lucky breaks and arbitrary advantages today that determine success—

the fortunate
birth dates and the
happy accidents
of history—with a
society that provides
opportunities
for all. "

MALCOLM GLADWELL

"You are the result of 3.8 billion years of evolutionary success. Act like it."

UNKNOWN

"The tragedy of life is not death, but what we let die inside of us while we live."

NORMAN COUSINS

"**Never ever be afraid to make some noise and get in good trouble, necessary trouble.**"

REP. JOHN LEWIS

GLOSSARY OF
PERSONS QUOTED

A.R. Bernard: Alfonso R. Bernard, Sr., pastor of Christian Cultural Center megachurch in Brooklyn, New York.

Abraham Lincoln: 16th president of the United States, serving from 1861 until his assassination in 1865.

Albert Einstein: German-born theoretical physicist known for developing the theory of relativity.

Hon. Alice M. Dear: former U.S. representative (ambassador) to the African Development Bank; president of A.M. Dear & Associates. A 2001 *Network Journal* honoree.

Antoine de Saint-Exupery: 20th Century French author and poet who documented his adventures as a pilot, most notably in *The Little Prince*.

Aristotle: philosopher and polymath in ancient Greece.

Arthur Ashe, Jr.: The first Black tennis player selected to the United States Davis Cup team; the only Black man ever to win the singles title at Wimbledon, the US Open, and the Australian Open.

Barbara Kushner: president and CEO of Armand Corporation, a construction management firm. A 2019 *Network Journal* honoree.

Basil King: Canadian clergyman who became an influential author of moral fiction.

Benjamin Franklin: a founding father of the United States and the first United States Postmaster General.

Billy Graham: American evangelist who became well known internationally in the late 1940s.

Bob Moawad: inspirational writer on human effectiveness; founder/chairman of Edge Learning Institute.

Charles "Chuck" Swindoll: evangelical Christian pastor, founder of Insight for Living.

Charles E. Shelton: father of 2015 *Network Journal* honoree Helen S. Shelton, senior partner, Multicultural, Luxury and Lifestyle Communications Strategist at Finn Partners Incorporated

Claude Thomas Bissell: Canadian author and educator.

Clayton Christensen: American academic, business consultant, architect of the theory of "disruptive innovation."

Colin Powell: four-star general (ret.). Son of Jamaican immigrants, he was the 65th and first African American U.S. Secretary of State, serving from 2001 to 2005.

Confucius: Chinese philosopher, teacher and political theorist whose teachings formed the basis of East Asian culture and society.

Dolly Parton: American country music singer/songwriter.

Dr. Seuss: pen name of Theodor Seuss Geisel, American children's author and cartoonist.

Duke Ellington: African-American composer and pianist deemed the greatest jazz composer and bandleader of his time.

Eleanor Roosevelt: first lady of the United States from 1933 to 1945, during her husband President Franklin D. Roosevelt's four terms in office.

Epictetus: Greek Stoic philosopher who was born a slave, lived in Rome, and returned to Greece after he was banished.

Erma Bombeck: newspaper columnist who wrote humorously about suburban American home life.

Erwin MacManus: author, filmmaker, fashion designer and lead pastor of Mosaic megachurch in Los Angeles.

George Bernard Shaw: Anglo-Irish playwright, political activist.

Gloria Steinem: leader of the American feminist movement in the late 1960s and early 1970s; founder of *Ms.* magazine.

Harriet Tubman: an escaped slave who helped others gain their freedom as a "conductor" of the Underground Railroad, earning her the title, "the Moses of her people." Reputedly the first African-American woman to serve in the U.S. military, she was a scout, spy, guerrilla soldier, and nurse for the Union Army during the American civil War.

Harry S. Truman: 33rd president of the United States, serving from 1945 to 1953.

Harvey Mackay: American businessman who authored several New York Times bestselling books, including *Swim With The Sharks Without Being Eaten Alive.*"

Helen Keller: American author and disability rights advocate who lost her sight and hearing from illness at the age of nineteen months.

Henry David Thoreau: American naturalist, essayist, poet, philosopher and leading transcendentalist,

Henry Ford: American industrialist; founder of the Ford Motor Company, and chief developer of the assembly line technique of mass production

Hillel: one of the best-known sages of the Talmud, the primary source of Jewish religious law and theology.

Hugh Sidney: American journalist who covered U.S. presidents from Dwight D. Eisenhower to William "Bill" Clinton.

Jack Welch (John Francis Welch, Jr.): chairman and CEO of General Electric from 1981 to 2001.

Jackie Joyner-Kersee: African-American track and field athlete, ranked among the all-time greatest in the heptathlon and long jump.

Jacqueline W. Sales: founder and president of HAZMED, an environmental engineering and information technology consulting firm. A 2003 Network Journal honoree.

James Keller: 20th Century American Roman Catholic priest in the Maryknoll Order who founded The Christophers, a Christian inspirational group.

Jennifer Lee: American screenwriter, film director, and chief creative officer of Walt Disney Animation Studios.

Joan M. Prince, Ph.D.: vice chancellor of The University of Wisconsin-Milwaukee, a 2020 *Network Journal* honoree.

Johann Wolfgang von Goethe: considered the greatest German literary figure of the modern era.

John Maxwell: American author and pastor, considered America's No. 1 authority on leadership and one of the world's most popular on the subject.

Joli C. Cooper: founding partner of Cordova, Smart & Williams LLC, a private equity investment firm. A 2007 *Network Journal* honoree.

Katherine Giscombe, Ph.D.: senior director of research at Catalyst, a 2005 *Network Journal* honoree.

Khalil Gibran: Lebanese-American writer, poet and visual artist.

Lisa A. Bing: president of Bing Consulting Group Inc., a business strategy and leadership enhancement firm. A 2007 *Network Journal* honoree.

Lou Holtz: former American football player, coach, and sports analyst.

M.A. Stodart: 19th century British author of books on female education.

Mac Anderson: American founder of Simple Truths and Successories, Inc., which designs and markets products for motivation and recognition.

Madeleine Albright: first female U.S. Secretary of State, serving from 1997 to 2001 under President Bill Clinton.

Mahatma Gandhi: Indian lawyer, anti-colonial nationalist and political ethicist who used nonviolence to successfully campaigned for India's independence from British rule.

Malcolm Gladwell: Canadian author, journalist and public speaker. Son of Jamaican and English parents, he is considered one of the world's most influential thinkers.

Margaret Thatcher: prime minister of the United Kingdom from 1979 to 1990.

Maria L. Johnson: former vice president of Diversity, Health and Work Life Initiatives at Fannie Mae, a 2003 *Network Journal* honoree.

Marian Wright Edelman: African-American activist for children's rights; founder and president emerita of the Children's Defense Fund.

Marianne Williamson: American author, spiritual leader and peace activist, best known as Oprah Winfrey's "spiritual adviser."

Martin Luther King, Jr.: African-American Baptist minister who became the most visible spokesman and leader in the civil rights movement from 1955 until his assassination in 1968.

Mary Engelbreit: American artist whose illustrations have been printed in books, cards and calendars.

Max Ehrmann: American writer, poet, and attorney, widely known for his 1927 prose poem "Desiderata."

Maya Angelou: African American poet, memoirist, and civil rights activist.

Michelangelo: Italian sculptor, painter, architect and poet of the High Renaissance.

Miguel de Cervantes: Spanish writer considered the greatest writer in the Spanish language. Best known for his novel, *Don Quixote*.

Muhammad Ali: African American professional boxer and activist, widely regarded as one of the most significant and celebrated figures of the 20th century, and ranked the best heavyweight boxer of all time.

Napoleon Hill: American self-help author, best known for his book *Think and Grow Rich* which is among the 10 best-selling self-help books of all time.

Nelson Mandela, 1918-2013: South African anti-apartheid revolutionary, statesman and philanthropist who served as President of South Africa from 1994 to 1999. He was the country's first black head of state and the first elected in a fully representative democratic election.

Nora Roberts: American romance novelist.

Norman Cousins: American political journalist, author, professor, and world peace advocate.

Oprah Winfrey: African American billionaire talk show host, television producer, actress, author, and philanthropist.

Patrick Overton, Ph.D.: American poet, author, ordained minister in the Christian church, founder of The Front Porch Institute.

Paulo Coelho: Brazilian songwriter and novelist.

Philip Yancey: American author who writes mostly about spiritual issues.

Phyllis G. Wooley: former director of African American Marketing for Colgate-Palmolive Company. A 2001 *Network Journal* honoree.

Ralph Bunche: American diplomat; member of the U.S. delegation to the United Nations; winner of the Nobel Peace Prize in 1950, making him the first African American to be awarded a Nobel Prize.

Ralph Waldo Emerson: American essayist, lecturer, philosopher, abolitionist and poet who led the transcendentalist movement of the mid-19th century.

Randal Pinkett, Ph.D.: serial entrepreneur, Rhodes Scholar, author; co-founder, chairman and CEO of BCT partners, a multimillion-dollar management, technology and policy consultancy; first African American to win the reality television show *The Apprentice*.

Rep. John Lewis: African American civil rights activist who represented Georgia's 5th congressional district in the US House of Representatives from 1987 until his death in 2020.

Ronald Harmon Brown: father of 2016 *Network Journal* honoree Tracey L. Brown, Esq., managing partner at The Cochran Firm-New York.

Richard Carlson: American actor, television and film director, and screenwriter.

Rosalynn Carter: first lady of the United States from 1977 to 1981 as the wife of President Jimmy Carter.

Sandra Bookman: African-American anchor and reporter for WABC-TV. A 2013 *Network Journal* honoree.

Seneca: Roman philosopher, dramatist and statesman who served as an adviser to Emperor Nero.

Shirley Chisholm: American politician, educator, and author. Daughter of Guyanese and Barbadian immigrants, she was the first Black woman elected to the United States Congress and the first woman to ruin for president of the United States.

Sir Winston Churchill: prime minister of the United Kingdom 1940-1945 and again from 1951-55.

Steve Jobs: American business magnate, industrial designer, investor, and media proprietor, best known as co-founder, chairman and chief executive of Apple Inc.

Teneshia Jackson Warner: CEO of Egami Group, a marketing firm that links top brands to urban consumers. A 2019 *Network Journal* honoree.

The Secret: a 2006 documentary and subsequent bestselling book by Rhonda Byrne that revealed the great mystery of the universe.

The Serenity Prayer: a prayer written by American theologian Reinhold Niebuhr.

Theodore Roosevelt: The 26th president of the United States, serving from 1901 to 1909.

Thomas Paine: American political activist, philosopher, and political theorist, best known as author of *Common Sense* and *The American Crisis* , the two most influential pamphlets at the start of the American Revolution.

Valorie Burton: African-American life coach, author, motivational speaker and entrepreneur; founder of the Coaching and Positive Psychology Institute.

Victor Frankl: Austrian neurologist, psychiatrist and philosopher; founder of logotherapy, a school of psychotherapy that describes a search for a life meaning as the central human motivational force.

Vince Lombardi: American football coach and National Football League executive.

Vivian Greene: American artist, author, entrepreneur; adviser to business moguls and major corporations on balancing the highest good with the bottom line.

W.A. (William Arthur) Ward: American motivational writer.

Washington Irving: American short-story writer, essayist, historian, and diplomat; best known for his short stories *Rip Van Winkle* and *The Legend of Sleepy Hollow*.

Whitney Young, Jr.: American civil rights leader; executive director, and president of the national Urban League from 1961 to 1971; recipient of the Presidential Medal of freedom from President Lyndon B. Johnson.

Wilma Mankiller: Cherokee activist, social worker, community developer and the first woman elected to serve as Principal Chief of the Cherokee Nation.

Biblical Quotations

Hebrews 11:1

Jeremiah 29:11

Luke, 12: 48-49

Philippians 4:6

Philippians 4:8

Philippians 4:11

Philippians 4:13

Proverbs 3:5-6

Ethnic Proverbs Quoted

African

Chinese

Native American

About
Rosalind Kilkenny McLymont

Rosalind Kilkenny McLymont is the executive editor of *The Network Journal* and the author of two fiction and two non-fiction works. Born in Guyana, she is a graduate of The City College of New York - CUNY and New York University, with a Certificate in Spanish Language and Literature from The Autonomous University of Madrid, Spain. A past European Union Fellow, she taught English and French in Uganda and the Democratic Republic of Congo; served as an entrepreneurship development expert for the Gender Program of United Nations Development Program's Africa Bureau; conducted professional development workshops in Russia with the Alliance of Russian and American Women to; and served two terms on the Sub-Saharan Africa Advisory Committee of the Export-Import Bank of the United States. She is a certified senior fitness instructor (International Fitness Association); a certified Zumba Gold® instructor; has a Black Belt and instructor training in Tai Chi, and instructor training in Qi Gong. She is the creator of "My Fabulous Me!" a self-acceptance workshop for women.